INSPIRED
to make a
difference
every day

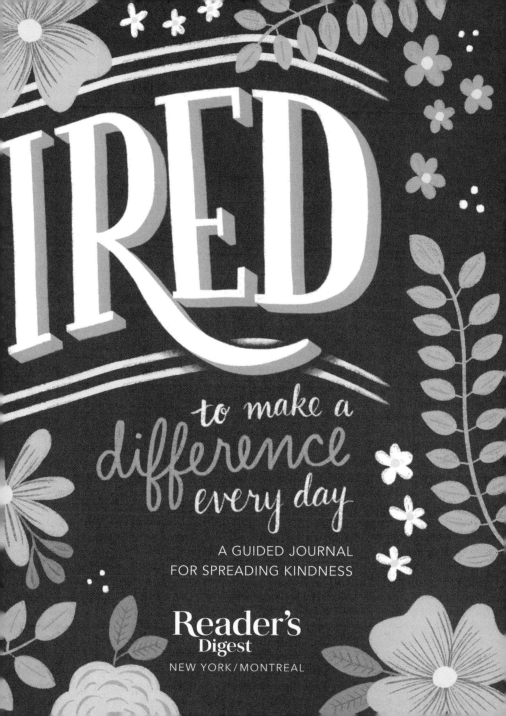

IRED

to make a
difference
every day

A GUIDED JOURNAL
FOR SPREADING KINDNESS

Reader's
Digest

NEW YORK / MONTREAL

INTRODUCTION

Lately, it might seem as if the world is hopelessly divided. Between social distancing and polarizing headlines, it's easy to feel disconnected. But we believe there's always room for hope. And that hope begins with each of us. Every day we have the opportunity to spread kindness—in our families, our communities, and the world around us. We can let people know they're not alone. We can remind friends why we love them. We can feed those who are hungry, compliment a stranger, support a local business, and learn more about ourselves and others. We can change the world around us, one thoughtful action at a time.

Inside these pages you'll find more than sixty ideas for spreading kindness to friends, family and strangers; helping the environment; giving back to your community; and focusing on what unites instead of divides us. You'll also find inspiring quotes from artists, thinkers, musicians, and leaders, as well as real-life stories of friendship and compassion from readers like you. And we've included space for reflecting on each of these actions, so that you can see the difference you made and be inspired to continue this journey of giving back. Finally, at the end of the book, we've included several of our favorite resources to help you learn more and do more. We hope you'll continue to add to this list as you strive to make this world a little bit better.

We created this journal because we know that simple acts of kindness can make meaningful change. Together, we can be inspired to make a difference every day.

—The Editors of *Reader's Digest*

TO
REMEMBER
Friendship

IS TO RECALL THOSE

CONVERSATIONS

THAT IT SEEMED A SIN TO BREAK OFF:
THE ONES THAT MADE THE SACRIFICE
OF THE FOLLOWING DAY A TRIVIAL ONE.

— *Christopher Hitchens*

PLAY SMARTPHONE ROULETTE.

SCROLL THROUGH YOUR CONTACT LIST
AND CALL THE FIRST PERSON WHOSE
NAME YOU SEE.

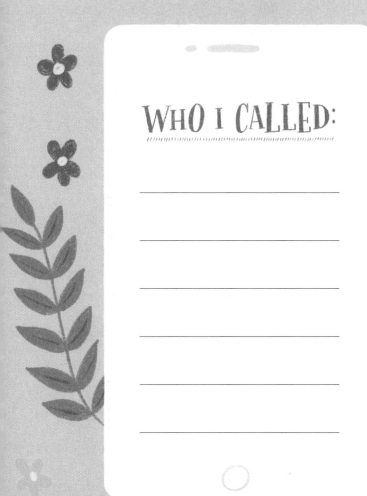

WHO I CALLED:

THERE ARE A LOT OF THINGS HAPPENING THAT SHOW US THAT THIS, RIGHT NOW, IS A TIME TO

Love

— STEVIE WONDER

HELP THE HELPERS!

OFFER TO GROCERY SHOP OR PET SIT FOR A DOCTOR OR NURSE IN YOUR COMMUNITY.

THE DIFFERENCE I MADE:

_____

_____

_____

_____

_____

_____

_____

THE GUY ON THE BENCH

My mom uses a wheelchair. Our city has buses with wheelchair lifts, but they slow things down and drivers don't like that. They often say, "The lift is broken." One day, Mom was waiting at the bus stop while a man snored on a nearby bench. But when the driver made his lame excuse, the man on the bench awoke and yelled at the driver for his heartlessness toward this old, crippled lady. Ashamed, the driver "miraculously" discovered that the lift worked after all. My mom got on the bus, and the guy on the bench went back to sleep.

Ray Martin, Glendora, California

SMILE AT A STRANGER.

THE KINDNESS I SPREAD:

_____

_____

_____

_____

_____

_____

_____

_____

_____

Do your little bit of good where you are; it is those little bits of good put together that overwhelm the world.

—DESMOND TUTU

PLANT A TREE IN YOUR
BACKYARD OR IN
YOUR NEIGHBORHOOD.

PLACE A PHOTO OR DRAW
A PICTURE OF THE TREE HERE:

HOW

WONDERFUL
IT IS THAT NOBODY
NEED WAIT A SINGLE MOMENT
BEFORE STARTING TO
IMPROVE THE
WORLD.

—ANNE FRANK

VOLUNTEER FOR A SHIFT AT A
SOUP KITCHEN OR FOOD BANK.

THE DIFFERENCE I MADE:

_____

_____

_____

_____

_____

_____

_____

_____

a Lesson in Kindness

My third-grade teacher and I had a magical bond. She moved after that year, though, and we lost touch. Thirty-one years later, we reconnected through Facebook. I sent her a picture of a doll she'd bought me back then to prove I'd kept it all this time. She immediately sent me a picture of the same doll! Turns out, she'd bought two dolls because they looked like her "little Jill" and she'd kept one to remember me by. Unknowingly, we'd both also named the doll Rebecca. You never know whose life you're going to impact in profound ways!

Jill Beeckman, Freeland, Michigan

WRITE A LETTER TO A FORMER TEACHER,
SHARING THE DIFFERENCE THAT PERSON
MADE IN YOUR LIFE.

TEACHER _____

GRADE _____

THOUGHTS I SHARED:

_____

_____

_____

_____

_____

_____

_____

_____

IN A NUTSHELL

Loving

SOMEONE

IS ABOUT

GIVING NOT

RECEIVING

—Nicholas Sparks

BRING SOMEONE **FLOWERS.**

THE KINDNESS I SPREAD:

_____

_____

_____

_____

_____

_____

_____

_____

_____

I have found that among its other benefits, GIVING liberates the soul of the GIVER.

—Maya Angelou

DONATE USED BOOKS OR TOYS TO YOUR LOCAL COMMUNITY CENTER.

The Difference I Made:

_____

_____

_____

_____

_____

_____

_____

_____

THE BEST VICTORY

My son, Mark, volunteered to help Cherie, a young runner at a local Special Olympics. Cherie was happy and enthusiastic. Mark encouraged her, kept her calm, and helped her know when it was time to line up for her race. When the starting pistol sounded, she took off like a lightning bolt, leaving her fellow racers behind. As she neared the finish line, she stopped, turned around, and motioned for the other runners to hurry. She waited for them so they could all cross the finish line together.

Debra Holley, American Fork, Utah

PARTICIPATE IN A
CHARITY WALK OR RACE.

EVENT: _____

DATE: _____

DETAILS: _____

_____

_____

_____

_____

_____

IF YOU DON'T GET
OUT ◆ BOX
OF
THE

YOU'VE BEEN RAISED IN,
YOU WON'T UNDERSTAND
HOW MUCH
BIGGER
THE WORLD IS.

— ANGELINA JOLIE

BROADEN YOUR WORLD VIEW!
LIST THE CULTURAL CENTERS IN
YOUR COMMUNITY—AND THEN VISIT
ONE OR ALL OF THEM, EITHER IN
PERSON OR ONLINE.

CULTURAL CENTERS NEAR ME:

_____

_____

_____

_____

_____

_____

_____

No one is useless in this world who lightens the burdens of another.

— CHARLES DICKENS

EASE SOMEONE'S LOAD.
DO A LOVED ONE'S LAUNDRY OR
OTHER HOUSEHOLD CHORE.

Butterfly Effect

My stepdaughter Pamela, a veterinarian, was visiting her aunt when they noticed a butterfly flying erratically around the room. Cupping it gently in her hands, Pamela realized a quarter of its wing was missing. While Auntie held the wings still on a table with toothpicks, Pamela performed surgery with scissors and contact cement. She fashioned a tiny prosthesis from a napkin and gently attached it to the wing. A minute later, the creature fluttered out a nearby window. While the two women congratulated each other, the butterfly reentered the room, flew around, and landed directly over Pamela's heart.

Robert McCormick, Kings Beach, California

DONATE BLANKETS OR TOWELS
TO AN ANIMAL SHELTER.

WHERE I DONATED:

_____

_____

_____

WHAT I GAVE:

_____

_____

_____

_____

_____

ONE OF THE
FIRST CONDITIONS
OF HAPPINESS IS
THAT THE LINK
BETWEEN MAN AND
NATURE SHALL
NOT BE BROKEN.

– LEO TOLSTOY

CLEAN UP A LOCAL
BEACH OR PARK.

place a photo of the cleaned-up location here:

ALL
IN THE
FAMILY

Upon attempting to prepare my seven-year-old daughter for a new baby in a few months, she repeatedly stated, "No boys in our house!" After several months, the BIG day arrived. My daughter came into the hospital room and I told her the baby was a boy and asked her, "What are we going to do?" She placed both her hands on her hips and without missing a beat said, "I guess we'll have to love the little thing!"

Karen Dugger, West Plains, Missouri

SAY ONE THING YOU **LOVE** ABOUT EACH FAMILY MEMBER:

READING

gives us someplace to go when we have to stay where we are.

—MASON COOLEY

VOLUNTEER TO READ AT AN ELEMENTARY SCHOOL OR LOCAL LIBRARY, EITHER IN PERSON OR ONLINE.

WHAT I READ:

_____

WHO I READ TO:

_____

HOW THEY RESPONDED:

_____

_____

_____

_____

Food for Thought

Recently I was reminded of something from sixty years ago. We had been married a little over a year, and I didn't know much about cooking. Bill wanted chicken and dumplings. At nineteen, I had no idea how to fix that. We were new to the area and didn't know anybody. So, I just dialed a random phone number in our area and explained my situation. The lady on the other end didn't miss a beat. She explained in detail. I must have listened well. Bill thought it was great!

Carmelita Pile, Los Angeles, California

SHARE A FAVORITE RECIPE
WITH A FRIEND OR ACQUAINTANCE.

MY RECIPE:

_____

_____

_____

_____

_____

_____

_____

_____

_____

ASSUMPTIONS ARE THE TERMITES OF RELATIONSHIPS.

—HENRY WINKLER

LEARN ABOUT A RELIGION OR
SPIRITUAL PATH WITH WHICH YOU ARE
UNFAMILIAR. EXPERIENCE A SERVICE,
EITHER VIRTUALLY OR IN PERSON.

SERVICE I ATTENDED:

_____

WHAT I LEARNED:

_____

_____

_____

_____

_____

_____

_____

One of the secrets of a long and fruitful life is to forgive everybody everything every night before you go to bed.

—ANN LANDERS

RIGHT A WRONG. APOLOGIZE TO SOMEONE YOU HAVE HURT. THEN, THINK OF SOMEONE WHO HAS HURT YOU—AND WRITE THAT PERSON A LETTER OF FORGIVENESS.

THE DIFFERENCE I MADE:

_____

_____

_____

_____

_____

_____

_____

BETTER TOGETHER

When I was a little girl, my father always let me help him with car and home repairs. Afterwards he used to say, "I couldn't have done it without you!" If he deemed a job too dangerous, he would seat me out of harm's way and have me read poetry aloud to him. He insisted this eased his work and would thank me just the same. I didn't write my own poetry until my father's last years. Now I have two published poetry collections and several awards. I couldn't have done it without YOU, Dad!

Laura Grace Weldon, Litchfield, Ohio

BE A ROLE MODEL.
SPEND THE AFTERNOON
WITH A CHILD.

Sharing the Love

A restaurant supplier of sushi-grade fish here in El Segundo unfortunately lost all of their orders, nearly overnight, as a result of the COVID-19 pandemic. They posted on my local nextdoor.com page that they were going to try selling directly to us locals at discounted rates, so some of us bought some. It was the best fish I had ever purchased, rivaling sushi that I've eaten in Japan. I posted a photo of their fish to reddit.com, mentioning their story. It got 4,000 upvotes and over 80 people reached out to me asking how to purchase fish from them. Here we are, weeks later, and while they still don't have any restaurant orders, they've been kept afloat by all of the new customers they gained from word of mouth and through these sites.

Jordan Spence, El Segundo, California

WRITE A GLOWING REVIEW
OF A LOCAL BUSINESS.

MY FIVE-STAR REVIEW:

_____

_____

_____

_____

_____

TRUE *Giving* HAPPENS WHEN WE GIVE FROM OUR *Heart.*

—Muhammad Ali

42

OH, BABY!

On a recent flight, I sat next to a mom with a baby on her lap and a slightly older son. She was having trouble holding on to the baby while helping her son and herself, so I offered to hold the baby. Baby and I hit it off right away—so much so that when Mom reached to take her back, Baby started screaming! So Mom left her with me. For two hours, we played tickle and moved the tray table up and down. After we landed, I handed the baby back. Mom smiled and said, "Thank you!"

Raymond Drago, Glen Mills, Pennsylvania

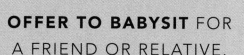

OFFER TO BABYSIT FOR
A FRIEND OR RELATIVE.

THE KINDNESS I SPREAD:

A SINGLE ACT OF

KINDNESS

THROWS OUT

ROOTS

IN ALL DIRECTIONS,
AND THE ROOTS SPRING UP
AND MAKE NEW TREES.

—Amelia Earhart

COMPLIMENT
A STRANGER.

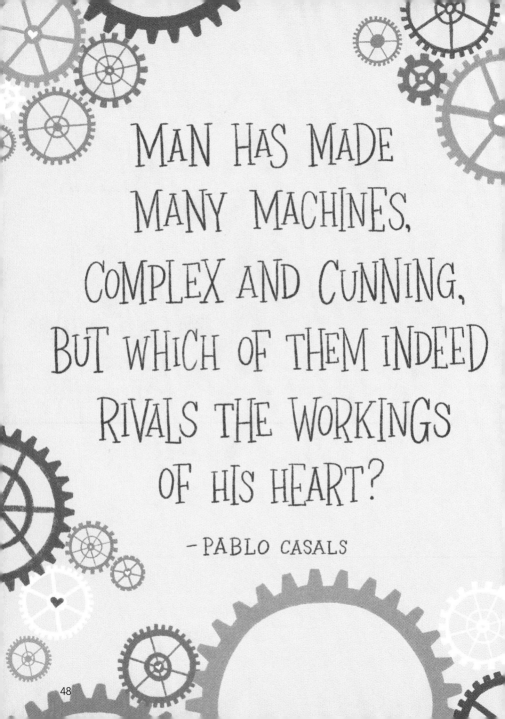

MAN HAS MADE
MANY MACHINES,
COMPLEX AND CUNNING,
BUT WHICH OF THEM INDEED
RIVALS THE WORKINGS
OF HIS HEART?

−PABLO CASALS

GIVE YOUR FAMILY AND FRIENDS
THE **GIFT OF YOUR PRESENCE.**
GO SCREEN-FREE FOR A DAY.

MY SCREEN-FREE EXPERIENCE:

_____

_____

_____

_____

_____

_____

_____

_____

a Fair Deal

My son-in-law Chuck shovels driveways for several clients in the winter. Once while he was shoveling, a little old lady came by and asked if he could do her driveway too. Chuck agreed. When he finished, she asked him how much she owed him. Chuck told her "twenty-five." She went into the house, came back out, and gave him a quarter. She then asked if he was sure that was enough. Chuck just smiled and said, "Yeah, I guess that is good." He kept clearing the snow from her driveway for "twenty-five" until she passed away recently.

Jean Litke, Pierz, Minnesota

HELP AN ELDERLY NEIGHBOR

WITH A CHORE, SUCH AS SHOVELING HER
DRIVEWAY OR BRINGING HIM GROCERIES.

THE DIFFERENCE I MADE:

_____

_____

_____

_____

_____

_____

_____

to say my fate
is not tied to your fate
is like saying:

YOUR END OF
THE BOAT IS
SINKING.

– Hugh Downs

START A RECYCLING PROGRAM
AT YOUR SCHOOL OR OFFICE.

an open mind

Jerry was the security guard at my school. He was a silent, stoic old man who scolded us when we ran down halls. Other students called him "Scary Jerry" when out of his earshot. He looked retirement age; I wondered why he stayed at the school among such unfriendly people. Ben was a boy with autism in my grade. Everybody loved his sweet, charming personality. One day, I was walking in the hall and saw Jerry and Ben talking. I saw Ben hug Jerry and call him "Daddy." I finally realized why Jerry stayed at the school.

Rachel Shin, Mechanicsburg, Pennsylvania

GET TO KNOW SOMEONE YOU MAY HAVE JUDGED PREMATURELY. INVITE HIM TO COFFEE, SIT WITH HER IN CLASS, OR FIND TIME TO CHAT TOGETHER IN THE OFFICE BREAK ROOM.

THE DIFFERENCE I MADE:

_____

_____

_____

_____

_____

_____

_____

KINDNESS

IS NEVER WASTED.
IF IT HAS NO EFFECT
ON THE RECIPIENT,
AT LEAST IT BENEFITS
THE BESTOWER.

— S.H. SIMMONS

LET SOMEONE **GO IN FRONT**
OF YOU IN LINE.

WRITE
INJURIES
IN
SAND,

kindnesses

IN
MARBLE.

— FRENCH PROVERB

STOP THE CYCLE OF NEGATIVITY.
RESPOND TO CRITICISM OR RUDENESS
WITH KINDNESS AND RESPECT—WHETHER
IN PERSON OR ON SOCIAL MEDIA.

THE KINDNESS I SPREAD:

_____

_____

_____

_____

_____

_____

_____

_____

Mother's Helper

One morning, I jokingly told my husband he dropped the ball because he didn't make me coffee and I was having trouble getting motivated to start the day. My five-year-old son overheard me and asked me to explain what "dropped the ball" meant. A few minutes later, he came into our bedroom holding an overflowing coffee mug with a dishcloth underneath it to catch the drips. He said to my husband, "You dropped the ball, but I picked the ball up," and he handed me the worst tasting, most watered down, but sweetest cup of coffee ever.

Jennifer Stockberger, Mount Vernon, Ohio

MAKE A MEAL FOR A SICK
FAMILY MEMBER OR FRIEND.

NEVER, EVER BE AFRAID TO MAKE SOME NOISE & GET IN

good trouble,

NECESSARY

TROUBLE.

— JOHN LEWIS

CALL OR WRITE YOUR LOCAL LEGISLATOR ABOUT AN ISSUE THAT IS IMPORTANT TO YOU.

THE CHANGE I WANT TO SEE:

SERVING
with
PRIDE

A group of uniformed servicemen were exiting a restaurant as I entered with a group of teacher friends wearing our school shirts. I thanked them for serving our country and as they walked away, I heard one say, "They're the ones who work in a war zone full of runny noses, stacks of papers, and a thousand questions a day. I prefer my job!" Coming from a military family, I was both humbled and amused by our mutual admiration.

Stephanie Woodard, Missouri City, Texas

SEND A THANK-YOU NOTE
OR CARE PACKAGE TO
A SERVICEMEMBER.

LIFE'S MOST PERSISTENT
AND URGENT QUESTION IS
"WHAT ARE
YOU DOING
FOR OTHERS?"

—MARTIN LUTHER KING, JR.

OFFER TO MENTOR SOMEONE AT WORK
OR TUTOR SOMEONE AT SCHOOL.

THE DIFFERENCE I MADE:

OUR GOAL

MUST BE

DECENCY &

RESPECT

FOR EVERY

HUMAN WE

ENCOUNTER.

—OPRAH WINFREY

MAKE A LIST OF BOOKS IN WHICH
AUTHORS OF DIFFERENT BACKGROUNDS—
SUCH AS RACE, RELIGION, OR SEXUAL
ORIENTATION—SHARE THEIR EXPERIENCES.
AS YOU READ THEM, DISCUSS THESE BOOKS
WITH YOUR FRIENDS AND FAMILY.

My Reading List:

_____

_____

_____

_____

_____

_____

_____

a Class Act

I was having the time of my life with the incredible fifth-grade class I had this year. They were full of compassion and creativity. One day a student raised her hand and asked if I had realized I was wearing two different shoes. Laughter filled the room and I blushed with embarrassment. The next gesture is the part I will never forget: The students proceeded to trade shoes with each other to match my crazy situation.

Teresa Kiefer, Genoa City, Wisconsin

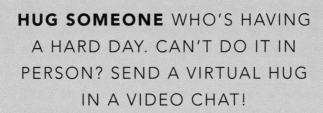

HUG SOMEONE WHO'S HAVING A HARD DAY. CAN'T DO IT IN PERSON? SEND A VIRTUAL HUG IN A VIDEO CHAT!

THE MOST
IMPORTANT
TRIP YOU MAY
TAKE IN LIFE IS
MEETING PEOPLE
HALFWAY.

—HENRY BOYE

THINK OF SOMEONE YOU FREQUENTLY DISAGREE WITH—ABOUT POLITICS, RELIGION, ETC.—AND MAKE A LIST OF ALL THE THINGS YOU HAVE IN COMMON. REACH OUT TO THAT PERSON WITH A KIND WORD.

what we have in common:

_____

_____

_____

_____

GIVING BACK

While sitting in the waiting room to donate blood, another patient was called before me, out of turn. As I sat there irritated, I overheard a young couple. The wife's iron count was too low to donate for her baby who was having surgery the next day. I got up and went over to the mom. I said, "I'll donate for your baby." I knew I could as I'm type O negative. If I had been called in turn, I would have never heard the story. My irritation turned to joy for this family.

Linda Tipon, San Diego, California

SAVE A LIFE. DONATE BLOOD
OR PLASMA OR HELP ORGANIZE
A BLOOD DRIVE.

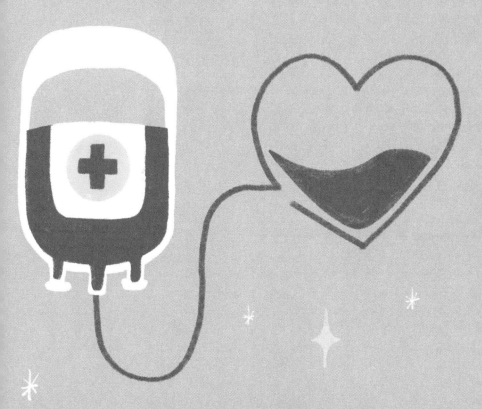

A small body
of determined spirits
fired by an unquenchable
faith in their mission can
alter the course of history.

–MOHANDAS GANDHI

START A PETITION FOR A CAUSE THAT
HAS SPECIAL MEANING FOR YOU.

My Petition:

_____

_____

_____

_____

_____

BIRDS *of a* FEATHER

On a self-imposed COVID-19 isolation, I felt increasingly depressed from living alone. After a long, spiritless walk, I remembered to feed the birds before settling in for the evening. Loading the feeder, I noticed a chickadee (my favorite bird) alighting on a nearby branch, waiting expectantly. As I stepped away, the bird flew to the feeder, pausing on a perch. Looking me straight in the eye, it sang a high-pitched "cheep, cheep," then grabbed a seed and flew off— a thank-you I'll never forget! Tears welling up, I knew God had not forgotten me. His little messenger reminded me of that.

David Gregorski, Coventry, Connecticut

CALL SOMEONE WHO IS GOING THROUGH A DIFFICULT TIME AND REALLY LISTEN.

THE KINDNESS I SPREAD:

_____

_____

_____

_____

_____

_____

_____

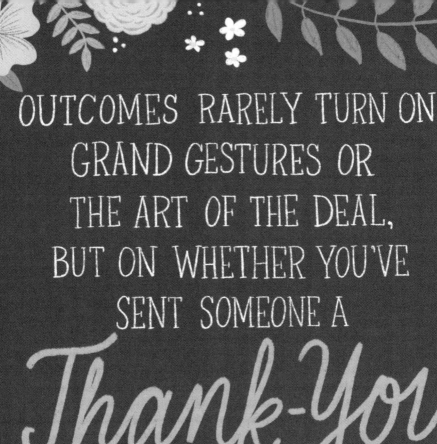

OUTCOMES RARELY TURN ON
GRAND GESTURES OR
THE ART OF THE DEAL,
BUT ON WHETHER YOU'VE
SENT SOMEONE A

Thank-You Note.

—BERNIE BRILLSTEIN

SEND A HOMEMADE GREETING CARD.

MY MESSAGE:

_____

_____

_____

_____

_____

_____

_____

FINDING Laughter

When I woke up, I knew it was cancer. The doctor's grim face combined with my mom's, who was trying so hard to smile for me, confirmed it. There would be surgery and treatment later, but I didn't want to wait. Groggy and weak from anesthesia, what could I do now? Make my mom laugh. I gestured to my abdomen. "Does this ... have anything to do with this?" I asked the doctor, sketching a circle over my premature bald spot, a running family joke. Silence, then Mom burst out laughing, breaking the dam. That's how I won the next year. Find laughter, then fight.

Andrew Elder, Albany, New York

MAKE SOMEONE LAUGH.
TELL A JOKE OR PASS ALONG
A FUNNY STORY.

LEADERS

DON'T CREATE

Followers,

THEY CREATE MORE

LEADERS.

—TOM PETERS

PRAISE A COLLEAGUE'S HARD WORK TO THE BOSS.

THE DIFFERENCE I MADE:

_____

_____

_____

_____

_____

_____

_____

_____

Love Notes

When my husband and I were dating, we visited the home of our friend's parents and I noticed a note on their refrigerator that read "Pete Loves Sue" (the parents' names). I told my then-boyfriend, Bruce, that I'd like to see a note like that on my refrigerator. A few days later, I approached my refrigerator and what did I see on the door—a note that read "Pete Loves Sue"! My husband and I have been married for twenty-five years and that joke has continued to show up, most recently on the screen of my phone.

Laura Payne, High Point, North Carolina

TAPE A KIND NOTE OR
SPECIAL PHOTO TO THE
FRIDGE TO LET A LOVED ONE
KNOW YOU CARE.

WHEN A GENERATION TALKS JUST TO ITSELF, IT BECOMES MORE FILLED WITH FOLLY THAN IT MIGHT HAVE OTHERWISE.

– STEWART BRAND

REACH OUT TO A LOCAL NURSING
HOME TO SEE HOW YOU CAN
VOLUNTEER—OR SEND A CARD OR
LETTER TO A SENIOR IN ITS CARE.

THE DIFFERENCE I MADE:

_____

_____

_____

_____

_____

_____

_____

An Unexpected GIFT

On my twenty-fourth birthday, I was standing a communications watch on the bridge of the USS *George Washington*. The captain was feared by the enlisted men and never spoke to anyone below officer status. It was early, and the sun was just appearing over the Mediterranean Sea. "Shipmate. Get over here!" the captain bellowed. "Yes, sir!" I ran from my alcove into view. "Look at that," he said, pointing to the red glowing sun cutting through the fog over the still, black sea. It was the most beautiful thing I had ever seen. I'll never forget his inadvertent birthday gift.

Michael Sutch, Sellersville, Pennsylvania

INVITE THE NEW PERSON AT
WORK OR SCHOOL TO LUNCH.

THE DIFFERENCE I MADE:

_____

_____

_____

_____

_____

_____

_____

_____

STRANGERS are Friends THAT YOU HAVE Yet to Meet.

—ROBERTA LIEBERMAN

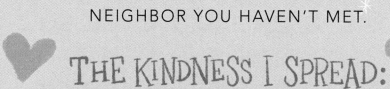

INTRODUCE YOURSELF TO A
NEIGHBOR YOU HAVEN'T MET.

THE KINDNESS I SPREAD:

Whenever you see darkness, there is extraordinary opportunity for the light to burn brighter.

–BONO

TAKE A CPR/FIRST AID COURSE.
IT MAY SAVE A LIFE.

FIRST AID CLASSES NEAR ME:

_____

_____

_____

_____

_____

_____

_____

_____

_____

THE KINDNESS OF STRANGERS

One month after we moved to the United States from halfway around the globe, I drove to Dulles International Airport near Washington, DC, with my wife to pick up her boss's guest. When we got back to the parking lot, our car was dead. It was an unexpected and embarrassing situation. Since we were new to the area, we were stuck. Then a gentleman who parked his car a few spots over came to help us jump our car. "Next time, it might be me in your position," he said. "Spread the love."

Shuai Tang, Arlington, Virginia

FEED SOMEONE'S
PARKING METER.

I DON'T BELIEVE IN E-MAIL. I'M AN OLD-FASHIONED GIRL. I PREFER CALLING AND HANGING UP.

— SARAH JESSICA PARKER

FIND SOMEONE ON YOUR SOCIAL MEDIA FEED YOU RARELY TALK TO OFFLINE, AND GIVE THAT PERSON A CALL.

WHO I CALLED:

I HAVE WITNESSED THE SOFTENING OF THE HARDEST OF hearts BY A SIMPLE SMILE.

— GOLDIE HAWN

HOLD THE DOOR
FOR SOMEONE.

THE KINDNESS I SPREAD:

_____

_____

_____

_____

_____

_____

_____

_____

_____

PAY IT FORWARD

I was third in line at the checkout and the lady at the cashier was purchasing basic items. Two cans of cat food, a can of tuna, a loaf of bread, a quart of milk, a package of cookies. Her money was in her hand as the cashier gave her the total. She was eighty-six cents short. She checked her purse to no avail. "I can put something back," she said. The man ahead of me reached into his pocket, palmed a dollar, bent down as if to pick something up, and said, "I think you dropped this." There is hope.

Michael F. Heberger, East Rochester, New York

BILLING STATEMENT

90 DAYS OVERDUE

PAY A BILL FOR A FRIEND
WHO'S FALLEN ON HARD TIMES.

BILLING STATEMENT

90 DAYS OVERDUE

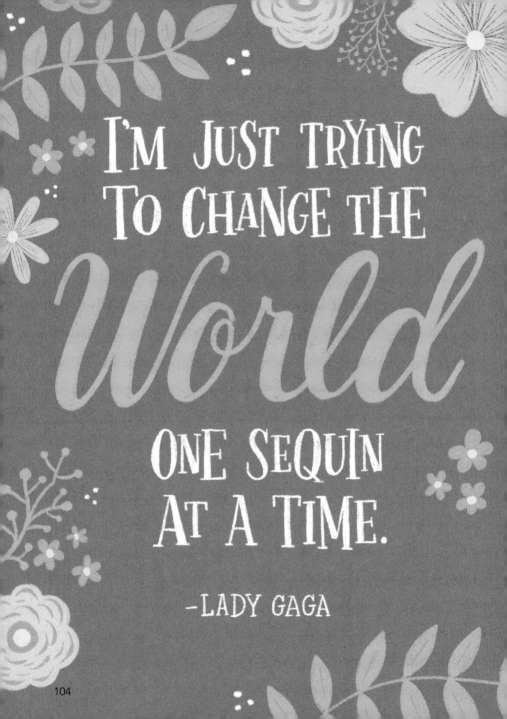

I'M JUST TRYING
TO CHANGE THE

World

ONE SEQUIN
AT A TIME.

–LADY GAGA

DONATE CLOTHES TO A LOCAL
THRIFT SHOP OR NONPROFIT.

CLOTHING DROP-OFFS NEAR ME:

_____

_____

_____

_____

_____

_____

_____

_____

YOU CANNOT TRULY SAY YOU

Live Well

UNLESS YOU

Eat Well.

— NIGELLA LAWSON

SUPPORT LOCAL FARMS.
BUY FROM A FARMERS' MARKET.

PLAY IT AGAIN

Our library had a "Music in the Lobby" day and I registered to play old-time piano tunes. An elderly gentleman and his granddaughter stopped to listen. Noticing he was unable to stand, I patted the bench alongside me and he took a seat. When I played "Strangers in the Night," he began to sing. An audience gathered as the man accompanied me throughout the recital. At the end, he was given a standing ovation. As the man left, his granddaughter whispered in my ear. "My grandpa has not sung a word since Grandma died," she said. "Thank you for giving him his voice back."

Lisa Leshaw, Coram, New York

MAKE A PLAYLIST FOR SOMEONE
WITH SONGS THAT MAKE YOU
THINK OF THAT PERSON.

A PLAYLIST FOR YOU:

_____

_____

_____

_____

_____

_____

_____

_____

THE SMALLEST DEED

IS

Greater

THAN THE

GRANDEST INTENTION.

—PATTI LaBELLE

LET SOMEONE INTO YOUR LANE IN TRAFFIC.

LEARNING TOGETHER

My eleven-year-old grandson and I meet once a week for lunch and homework. When he told me he felt stupid in math, I replied most people learning something new feel that way. We agreed to help each other—him with math and me with texting. He showed me how to text and then asked me to repeat what he taught. I completed the first two inputs and paused. He asked if I was having a problem. I told him I was just thinking about what to say. He replied, "That's easy, Gram. Just say I love you."

Muriel Smith, San Diego, California

TEACH A FAMILY MEMBER
A NEW SKILL.

THE DIFFERENCE I MADE:

_____

_____

_____

_____

_____

_____

_____

_____

What a wonderful thing is the mail, capable of conveying across continents a warm human hand-clasp.

— AUTHOR UNKNOWN

WRITE A THANK-YOU NOTE
TO YOUR MAIL CARRIER.

MY MESSAGE TO YOU:

we can deny
EVERYTHING
except that we have
the possibility of being
BETTER.

—THE DALAI LAMA

DONATE CREDIT CARD POINTS
OR UNUSED AIRLINE MILES
TO CHARITY.

WHAT I GAVE:

Woman's Best Friend

I saw him limping along, one rear leg dangling, useless, on my way home from work. He was a small, nearly hairless gray dog. I stopped and tossed him bits of bread to entice him closer. Leery, this broken little creature with stunning blue eyes let me put him in the car. My husband rebelled against $1,500 for surgery. "Take him to the pound!" he said. I did, but when he wrapped his paws around my arm in terror, I decided to face my husband's wrath. Now, six years later, he loves that little dog more than he loves me.

Lynn Adams, Santa Fe, New Mexico

ADOPT AN ANIMAL FROM
A SHELTER.

CERTIFICATE of ADOPTION

PET'S NAME

HAS FOUND HIS/HER FOREVER HOME

ON THE ___ DAY OF _____, 20 ___

CARRY OUT A RANDOM
ACT OF KINDNESS,
WITH NO EXPECTATION
OF REWARD, SAFE IN THE
KNOWLEDGE THAT ONE DAY
SOMEONE MIGHT DO THE
SAME FOR YOU.

—PRINCESS DIANA

RETURN A SHOPPING CART
LEFT IN THE PARKING LOT.

Success isn't about how much money you make, it's about the difference you make in people's lives.

—MICHELLE OBAMA

MAKE A LIST OF MORE GOOD DEEDS—
AND THEN GO DO THEM!

MY TO-DO LIST:

_____

_____

_____

_____

_____

_____

_____

RESOURCES

It's easier than ever to make a difference with all the resources available online these days! Here are a few of our favorite organizations and websites for spreading kindness every day.

American Red Cross
https://www.redcross.org/

Big Brothers Big Sisters of America
https://www.bbbs.org/

Earth Day: Take Action
https://www.earthday.org/take-action-now/

Habitat for Humanity
https://www.habitat.org/

The Salvation Army
https://www.salvationarmyusa.org/usn/

United Through Reading—Connecting Military Families
https://unitedthroughreading.org/